Thë Princëss öf Sapphirës and Sand

The Teacher's Edition
with Common Core Standards

Written by Tani Lamb
Illustrated by Pierre Mercieca

Dallas
Lamb Chop Publishing
2022

ISBN: 978-0-9983941-8-3 - Paperback

Library of Congress Control Number:

Printed in the United States of America
0 5 0 2 2 2

This paper meets the requirements of ANSI/NISO Z39.48-1992
(Permanence of Paper)

Cover Art and Illustrations by Pierre Mercieca

Published in the Dallas, Texas by
Lamb Chop Publishing
11700 Preston Rd Ste 660
#678
Dallas, Texas 75230
WWW.TANILAMB.COM
Edited by Booklogix in Atlanta, Georgia.

10 9 8 7 6 5 4 3 2 1

Dedication
To all of the educators persevering through these uncharted
educational times, thank you.

Princess of Sapphire and Sand Vocabulary List

AD (Anno Domini): The term used in the Christian calendar. AD is used to refer to a year after Jesus Christ was born.
CCSS.ELA-LITERACY.RH.6-8.4

Ancient Egypt: A civilization of ancient North Africa, concentrated along the lower reaches of the Nile River, situated in the place that is now the current Egypt.
CCSS.ELA-LITERACY.RL.7.3; CCSS.ELA-LITERACY. RH.6-8.4

Arabian Desert: A large desert located in Western Asia. The desert is 716,400 square miles. This makes it the largest desert in Asia. The Arabian Desert is the second largest desert in the world. The Sahara Desert in Africa is the largest desert.
CCSS.ELA-LITERACY.RL.8.4; CCSS.ELA-LITERACY. RL.7.3

BC: The term used in the Christian calendar. It stands for Before Christ, referring to a year before Jesus Christ was born.
CCSS.ELA-LITERACY.RH.6-8.4

BCE: Before Common Era
CCSS.ELA-LITERACY.RH.6-8.4

Bastet: The Egyptian goddess of cats, fertility, and childbirth. Bastet always carried a sistrum in her right hand. She protected the home and kept it safe from evil spirits and disease. Bastet also protected women and children from disease.

CCSS.ELA-LITERACY.RL.7.3; CCSS.ELA-LITERACY. RH.6-8.6

Big Ben: The nickname for the great bell within the striking clocktower at the north end of the Palace of Westminster. Big Ben was originally the name for just the bell. Now it is commonly used to mean both the clock and the clocktower.

C.E.: Common Era

CCSS.ELA-LITERACY.RH.6-8.4

Cleopatra's Needles: Four Egyptian obelisks from the Ancient Egypt. Two of the obelisks are originally from Heliopolis, Ancient Egypt. They were constructed in 1460 BC to celebrate the thirty-year reign of Pharaoh Thutmose III. In 525 BC, the obelisks were toppled and burned during an invasion by the Persian Empire. About five hundred years later, they were moved to Alexandria, Egypt, and were erected in front of the Caesareum. The Caesareum was a temple designed by Cleopatra VII. Cleopatra VII was the last pharaoh of Ancient Egypt. This may explain how these obelisks came to be known as "Cleopatra's Needles." The two obelisks from Alexandria, Egypt, are now on two different continents—one obelisk is in New York City in Central Park and the other obelisk is in London, England, on the Thames embankment. The final two obelisks are from Luxor, Egypt. The left-hand obelisk remains in its original location in Luxor, Egypt. The obelisk from the right-hand side now resides at the center of the Place de

Great Britain: An island separated from mainland Europe by two bodies of water, the English Channel and North Sea. The island of Great Britain contains the nations England, Scotland, and Wales.

CCSS.ELA-LITERACY.RL.7.3; CCSS.ELA-LITERACY. RL.6.4

The United Kingdom: The island of Great Britain plus the addition of Northern Ireland.

CCSS.ELA-LITERACY.RL.7.3; CCSS.ELA-LITERACY. RL.6.4

Griot: A member of a group of traveling poets, musicians, and storytellers who maintain a tradition of oral history. Griots are located in parts of West Africa

CCSS.ELA-LITERACY.RL.7.6; CCSS.ELA-LITERACY. RL.7.4

Isis: The Egyptian goddess of magic, fertility, and motherhood. She is also the goddess of death, rebirth, and healing.

CCSS.ELA-LITERACY.RH.6-8.4; CCSS.ELA-LITERACY. RL.7.6

Jinni (plural: Jinn): An intelligent spirit in Arabian and Muslim mythology. A Jinni is able to appear in the form of a human or animal. A jinni is also called a genie.

CCSS.ELA-LITERACY.RH.6-8.4; CCSS.ELA-LITERACY. RL.7.6

la Concorde in Paris, France.
CCSS.ELA-LITERACY.RL.8.4; CCSS.ELA-LITERACY.
RI.6.4

Egypt: A country located on the continent of Africa on
the Mediterranean Sea. Popular attractions in Egypt
are the Pyramids of Giza, the sphinx, the royal tombs,
mummies of ancient pharaohs, and the Suez Canal
CCSS.ELA-LITERACY.RH.6-8.4; CCSS.ELA-LITERACY.
RL.7.3; CCSS.ELA-LITERACY.RL.7.4

Eiffel Tower: Built by Gustave Eiffel, the tower was
designed as the centerpiece of the 1889 World's Fair
in Paris, France. This World's Fair celebrated the one-
hundredth-year anniversary of the French Revolution
CCSS.ELA-LITERACY.RL.7.3; CCSS.ELA-LITERACY.
RL.6.4

Falcon: A bird of prey, or a predator bird.
CCSS.ELA-LITERACY.RH.6-8.4

Falconry glove: A piece of safety equipment used in
falconry. The falconry glove turns the arm of the user
into a stable perching surface for the bird. The glove also
protects the user from the sharp talons of the bird.
CCSS.ELA-LITERACY.RL.7.4

Falconry: The hunting of wild animals in their natural
environment using a trained bird of prey. Small animals
such as rabbits are usually hunted.
CCSS.ELA-LITERACY.RH.6-8.4

London Eye: A Ferris wheel located in London, England, on the River Thames. The London Eye offers fantastic views of London.

CCSS.ELA-LITERACY.RI.7.4; CCSS.ELA-LITERACY.RI.6.3; CCSS.ELA-LITERACY.RI.6.4

London: The capital of England and the United Kingdom. London is home to the Houses of Parliament which is the center of the British government. Popular tourist attractions in London include the London Eye, Big Ben, the Tower of London, Tower Bridge, the British Museum, and Buckingham Palace with the changing of the guard.

CCSS.ELA-LITERACY.RL.7.3; CCSS.ELA-LITERACY.RL.6.4

Luxor: A modern Egyptian city on the Nile River. The famous Luxor Temple is located in Luxor. Luxor was part of the Ancient Egyptian city of Thebes.

CCSS.ELA-LITERACY.RH.6-8.4; CCSS.ELA-LITERACY.RL.7.3

Mediterranean Sea: A sea connected to the Atlantic Ocean. The Mediterranean Sea is surrounded by the land on three sides. The continent of Europe to the north, Northern Africa to the south, and the Levant (Western Asia) to the east.

CCSS.ELA-LITERACY.RH.6-8.4; CCSS.ELA-LITERACY.RH.6-8.5

New York City: Located in the state of New York, New York City has the largest population in the United States with over eight million people. The Dutch purchased

New York City from The Lenape Native Americans for about twenty-four dollars worth of traded goods. The Dutch then named the settlement New Amsterdam in 1653. The British conquered the area in 1664 and renamed it New York. Nicknames for New York City are the City that Never Sleeps, the Big Apple, and Gotham. Some of New York City's top tourist attractions are the Statue of Liberty, the Empire State Building, Central Park, Times Square, and the American Museum of Natural History

CCSS.ELA-LITERACY.RL.7.3; CCSS.ELA-LITERACY. RL.6.4

Obelisk: A Greek work for a pointed instrument. Obelisk is used to describe a monument that comes to a point at the top. The Washington Monument in Washington, DC, is an obelisk.

CCSS.ELA-LITERACY.RL.8.4

Paris: The capital city of France located on the Seine River. France is a country on the continent of Europe. Paris is also called the City of Light and the City of Love. Some famous tourist attractions in Paris include the Eiffel Tower, Notre Dame Cathedral, the Louvre, Champs-Élysées, and the Arc de Triomphe.

CCSS.ELA-LITERACY.RL.7.3; CCSS.ELA-LITERACY. RL.6.4

Persian Empire: Founded by Cyrus the Great around 550 BC, the Persian Empire became one of the largest empires in history. The Empire reached from Europe's Balkan Peninsula in the west to India's Indus Valley in the east. The Persian Empire built many new roads and developed the world's first postal service. The empire was also the first to establish regular channels of communication between the three continents of Africa, Asia, and Europe.

CCSS.ELA-LITERACY.RI.7.4; CCSS.ELA-LITERACY. RH.6-8.4

Piccadilly Circus: An intersection of roads and a public space of London's West End in the city of Westminster. It is a popular tourist attraction with neon signs, advertisements, theaters, retail shops, and restaurants. It was built in 1819 to connect Regent Street with Piccadilly. This circus is not for animals but from the Latin word meaning "circle." Piccadilly Circus is a round open space at the meeting of streets.

CCSS.ELA-LITERACY.RL.7.3; CCSS.ELA-LITERACY. RL.6.4

Pont des Arts Bridge Paris: A bridge in Paris, France, over the Seine River. Visitors attach locks with sentimental messages to the bridge in symbolic acts of love. The "locks of love" made the bridge too heavy and were eventually removed.

CCSS.ELA-LITERACY.RL.7.3; CCSS.ELA-LITERACY. RL.6.4

River Thames: A river that flows through southern England, including London. It is the longest river in England and the second-longest river in the United Kingdom. Along certain parts of the River Thames, it is also known as River Isis.

CCSS.ELA-LITERACY.RL.7.4

Scarab beetle: A large dung beetle from the eastern Mediterranean area. The scarab was important in ancient Egypt. The scarab represented the cycle of life and death and was often buried with pharaohs.
CCSS.ELA-LITERACY.RL.6.4

Sistrum: An ancient percussion instrument shaped like the letter U. The instrument was made of brass or bronze. There were rings which slid across the U-shaped body. The sound created when shaken was similar to a rattle.
CCSS.ELA-LITERACY.RH.6-8.4

Souvenir: An item kept as a reminder of something special.
CCSS.ELA-LITERACY.RL.6.4

Thebes: The capital city of Ancient Egypt from 1570–1069 BC. The modern area of Thebes now includes Luxor, the Valley of the Kings, the Valley of the Queens, and Karnak.
CCSS.ELA-LITERACY.RL.7.3; CCSS.ELA-LITERACY. RH.6-8.4

The British Empire: The largest empire to ever exist in history. The British Empire reached its height in 1913. In 1913, the empire covered twenty-five percent of the world's land surface. The empire had areas on North America, Australia, Africa, Asia, and South America. Twenty-three percent of the world's population was under the rule of the British Empire in 1913. The British

Empire began in the 1600s with colonies in the Americas. The first British settlement was Jamestown in 1607 under King James I.

CCSS.ELA-LITERACY.RI.7.4; CCSS.ELA-LITERACY. RH.6-8.4

The Levant: An area of western Asia on Mediterranean Sea. The Levant includes the countries of Lebanon, Syria, Iraq, Palestine, Israel, Cyprus, and Jordan.

CCSS.ELA-LITERACY.RL.7.4; CCSS.ELA-LITERACY. RL.7.3

The London Underground: Also called "The Tube," the Underground was the world's first underground railway system. The London Underground was established in 1863.

CCSS.ELA-LITERACY.RL.7.4

The Mongol Empire: The largest connected land empire in history. Only the British Empire had more landmass. The founder of the Mongol Empire was Genghis Khan. The Mongol Empire existed from AD 1206 to AD 1368 and dominated Asia.

CCSS.ELA-LITERACY.RI.7.4; CCSS.ELA-LITERACY. RH.6-8.4

The Nile River: The Nile is a major river in northeastern Africa. The river flows from south to north. The Nile is the longest river in Africa. The Nile River has historically been considered the longest river in the world.

CCSS.ELA-LITERACY.RL.7.3; CCSS.ELA-LITERACY.RL.7.4

The Palace of Westminster (or the Houses of Parliament): The meeting place of the House of Lords and the House of Commons. This is the center of the British Government. The most famous part of the building is the northern clocktower. The northern clocktower is now called the Elizabeth Tower. The Elizabeth Tower is the location of Big Ben.

CCSS.ELA-LITERACY.RL.8.4; CCSS.ELA-LITERACY.RI.8.3

Ticker Tape: The ribbon of paper on which stock price quotes appear in a long linear fashion. This long, white, thin paper provided stock market information to investors.

CCSS.ELA-LITERACY.RL.6.4

EUROPE

NORWAY

FINLAND

SWEDEN

POLAND

BELARUS

GERMANY

UKRAINE

ATLANTIC OCEAN

FRANCE

HUNGARY

ROMANIA

ITALY

BULGARIA

SPAIN

GREECE

MEDITERRANEAN SEA

MIDDLE EAST

NORTH AFRICA

⑬ ESTONIA
⑭ LATVIA
⑮ LITHUANIA
⑯ SLOVENIA
⑰ CROATIA
⑱ BOSNIA
⑲ SERBIA
⑳ MONTENEGRO
㉑ ALBANIA
㉒ MACEDONIA
㉓ MOLDOVA

① PORTUGAL   ⑦ LUXEMBOURG
② IRELAND   ⑧ SWITZERLAND
③ UNITED KINGDOM ⑨ DENMARK
④ ICELAND   ⑩ AUSTRIA
⑤ NETHERLANDS   ⑪ CZECH REP
⑥ BELGIUM   ⑫ SLOVAKIA

㉔ MALTA
㉕ CYPRUS

NORTH AMERICA

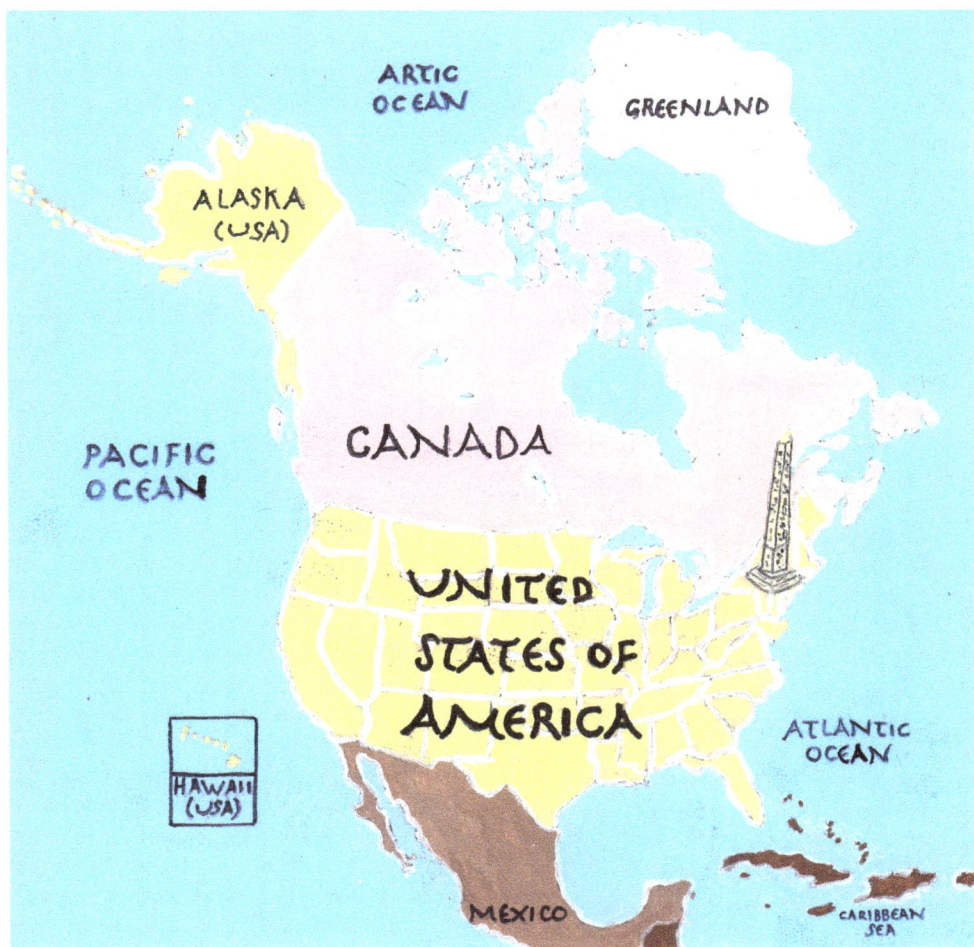

Northern Africa & the Middle East

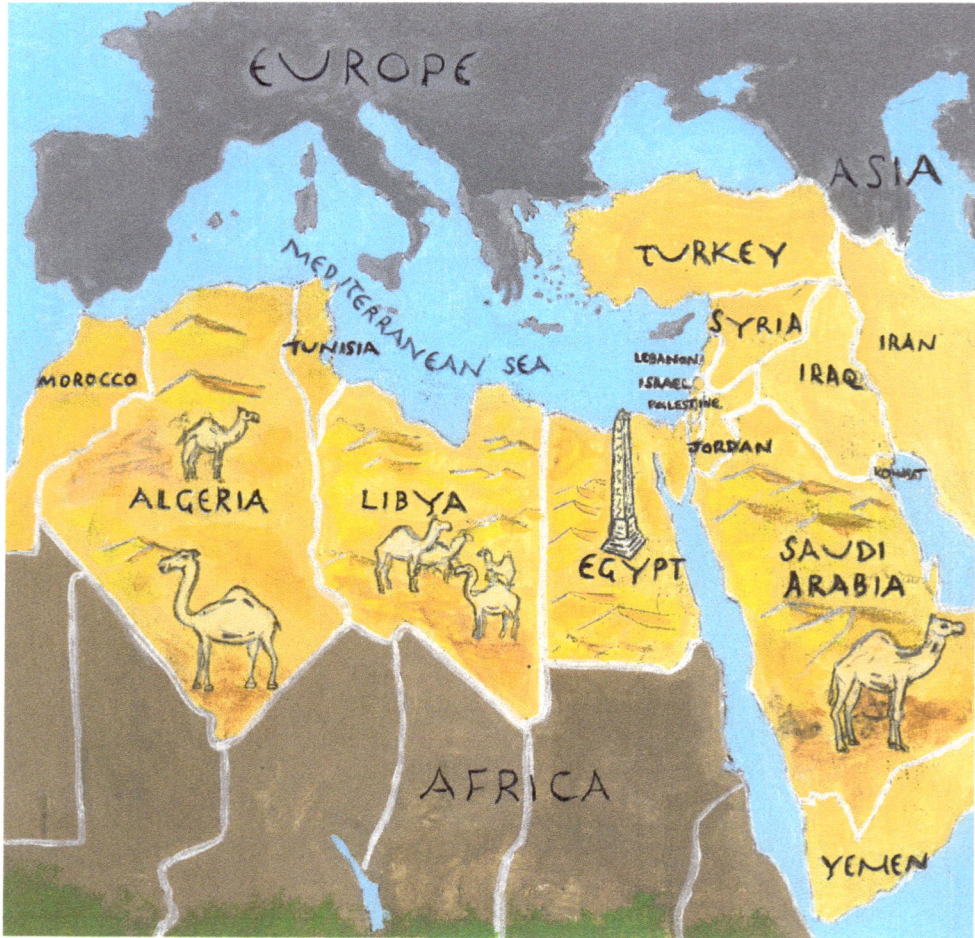

OMAN

MYRA

LUXOR, EGYPT

PARIS, FRANCE

LONDON, ENGLAND

LONDON, ENGLAND

New York City,
United States of America

THE MEDITERRANEAN

Acknowledgments

I would like to sincerely thank Pamela Thomas M.Ed. for providing her educational acumen and applying the common core learning objectives to the historical and geographical points of my book. Ms. Thomas earned her Bachelor of Arts in History and her Master of Arts in Curriculum and Instruction.

www.ingramcontent.com/pod-product-compliance
Lightning Source LLC
Chambersburg PA
CBHW052037030426
42337CB00027B/5042